IT'S A FACT
And It's Very Funny

One of the facts in this book is a blatant bogus — a fib if you like. See if you can tell which one it is: all the others are real but equally as strange as the bogus one. The answer is given at the end — but don't cheat, try to find it!

ITV BOOKS
in association with
MICHAEL JOSEPH

Published by

Independent Television Books Ltd
247 Tottenham Court Road
London W1P 0AU

In association with Michael Joseph Ltd

First published 1982
© Colin Hawkins 1982

ISBN 0 900727 97 7

Printed in Hong Kong by Aardvark Press

Many thanks to the ridiculous sense of humour of Jacqui, my wife,
John Doyle, Anna Selby, Joss Kelsey and Tony Selina.

IT'S A FACT
And It's Very Funny

Colin Hawkins

ITV BOOKS
in association with
MICHAEL JOSEPH

The most poisonous spider is the Brazilian wandering spider, who has an unfortunate penchant for hiding in people's shoes and clothing and biting their owners.

The world's largest spider, the bird-eating spider, has an extended leg span of a little more than 10½ in (26.6 cm) — thus making it larger than a dinner plate.

Eggshibitionist!

The African egg-eating snake can distend its jaws to over four times the circumference of its body. Once swallowed, the egg is broken by the internal spines of the backbone.

The smallest elephant was specially bred at 3ft (0.91m) tall.

The Kokoà frog of Colombia, South America, for protection secretes a poison so powerful that 0.1 milligrams is sufficient to kill a man.

People living in Elizabethan times rarely took baths. Elizabeth I regarded herself as a paragon of cleanliness. She declared she bathed once every three months — WHETHER SHE NEEDED IT OR NOT!

"We are no longer smelly."

The opossum is born in a very premature state and reared in the parent's pouch like a young kangaroo. A whole litter of 15 possums at birth could fit comfortably into an egg cup. The baby whale, on the other hand, is 24 ft (7.3m) long at birth and already bigger than an adult elephant.

...early 40,000 people ...e each year from snake ...es, three-quarters ...which are in India. ...e King Cobra causes ...e highest proportion ...deaths, and can even ...ll an elephant by striking ...the tender tip of ...s trunk.

sssss
chomp!

The tallest Irishman ever, was one
Patrick Cotter O'Brien of County Cork,
who at 8ft 1in (2.4m) matched
the height of a standard goalmouth
crossbar.

His enormous height had nothing
at all to do with the heaviest recorded
potato, at 7lb 1oz (3.2kg). This is
the average weight of a new-born
baby.

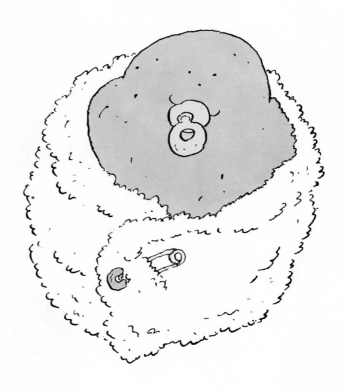

A horse called Napoleon was bred in Argentina that when fully grown was only 20 in (0.51m) tall, and weighed just 70 lb (31.8 kg).

Hedgehogs are marvellous swimmers, although they do not like the water much. They are also notorious carriers of fleas, and it's true that milk will attract them right up to your front door.

The world's heaviest hailstone fell in Kansas (USA) and was 1½ lb (0.68 kg) in weight and 17 in (43.18 cm) long.

Fleas can achieve high jumps of 7¾ in (19.68 cm) — 130 times their own height. For a man of 6ft (1.83m) this would mean a leap of 780ft (238m).

The world's fastest spider is capable of covering 33 times its own body length per second. If a 6ft man could do the same he would be able to sprint at a speed of 135mph (217km/h).

In 1939 at New York's World's Fair, one object of particular interest was an electric eel, who discharged a current that could run a miniature train, a radio and light up 300 neon bulbs.

To smarten up the circus elephant, his tough whiskers are shaved with blow lamp. His skin is too tough for him to feel anything at all.

"Down a bit.."

do like
news"
...Today at the New York Fair a radio and a fan were powered by Eelectricity...

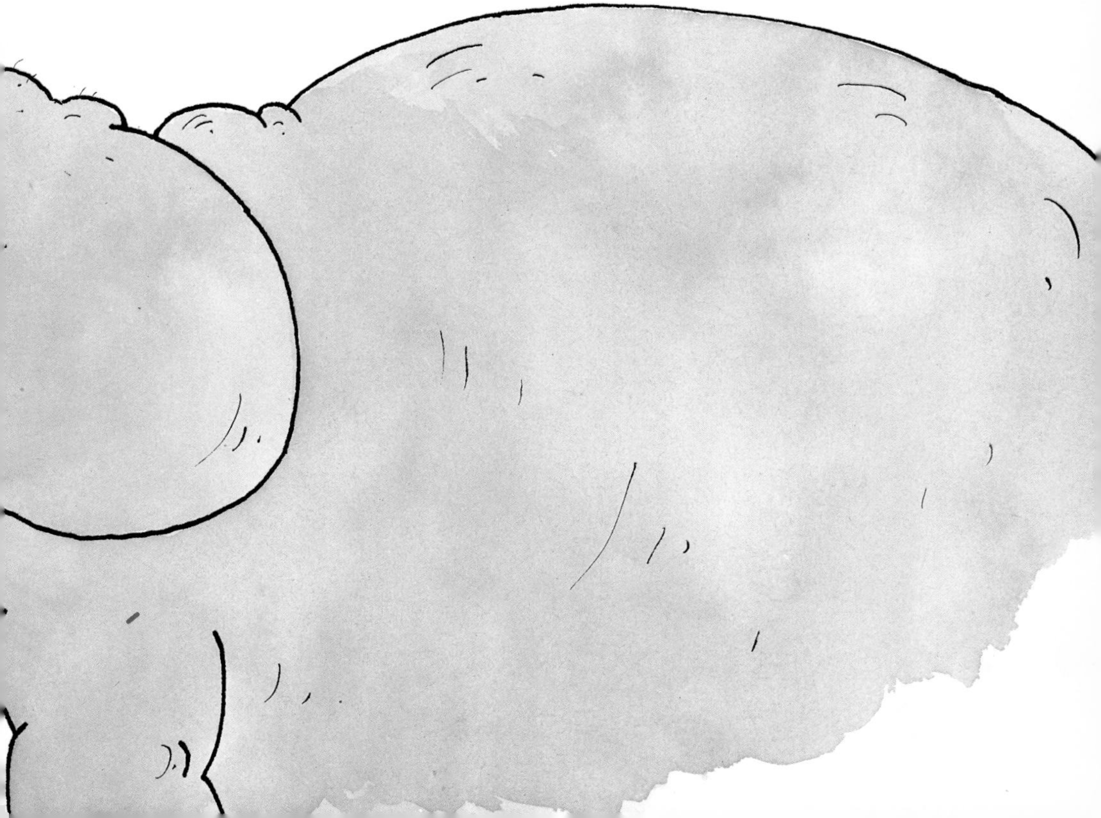

A snail going flat out would take eleven days to cover the distance of one mile (1.6 km).

The sloth, though enormously bigger, would take 19 days more than the snail to cover a mile. The sloth, moreover, is not an animal noted for its personal hygiene. For reasons of camouflage, it never washes and is consequently covered in green moss-like algae.

The Atlantic Giant Squid
can grow to a length of 55ft (16.76m),
weighing up to two tons.
It has the largest eyeball
of any known animal,
living or extinct,
which weighs several
pounds.

The greatest recorded overhead lift made by a woman was 286 lb (129.7 kg), slightly less than the weight of the average ostrich.

In 1972, a pigeon took two months to fly from London to South Africa — a distance of 6000 miles (9656 km) 'as the crow flies'. In fact, it probably flew 7,600 miles (12,231 km) to avoid the Sahara. The pigeon is the only bird able to draw in water and swallow in one go. Other birds have to throw their heads back after each sip.

we'll be seeing yooooooo""

There are regions of desert, in the Kalahari for instance, known as 'singing sands' because of the haunting sounds they produce.

The Roman Emperor Caligula — whose family was not noted for sweet reason — had probably the highest claim to madness of them all. Not satisfied with the family custom of conferring godhead upon the members of its noble house, he made his horse, Incitatus, consul and high priest.

...To days lesson is taken from...

..ecember 1980 a 78 lb (35.4 kg) turkey
.. the Heaviest Turkey Competition, held annually
..ondon. The Bedouin wedding breakfast makes
.. look paltry – they feast on roasted camel.

Horatio Nelson, England's most illustrious admiral, was never throughout his life able to find a cure for his sea-sickness.

An extremely rare spider exists in Leicester, England, which is able to secrete a web onto a wall, pull itself in and catapult out for distances of up to 10 ft (3.04 m).

The great English painter, J M Turner, had himself tied to the mast of a ship during a terrible storm so that, should he survive, he could recapture it on canvas. He was 67 at the time.

The fastest snake, the Black Mamba, could easily overtake any jogger unwise enough to find himself on the Serengeti Plains.

In certain parts of the world there are fish,
particularly members of the perch family, that
are able to, and do, climb trees.

He's quiet today!

The tallest skyscraper is the Sears Tower in Chicago at 1454 ft (443m). Yet birds have been reported flying at fifteen times that height, at 27,000ft (8230m), close to the top of Mount Everest.

The biggest bull recorded to date weighed in at precisely 5000 lb (2268 kg). His girth was 13 ft (3.9 m), the length of the inappropriately-named 'Mugger' crocodile— a beast so docile that it will ignore people who might walk about it.

The remarkable humming
bird of Cuba is 2¼ in
(5.71 cm) long, weighs
½ oz (14.17 gm), lays eggs
which are ¼ in (0.63 cm)
long and hatch birds
smaller than some insects.
The adults will fight
birds 4 or 5 times their
own size.

11st

The giant water-lily of Brazil has pads 6ft (1.83m)
in diameter that are sufficiently strong for ten stone
(63.5 kg) adults to use them as rafts.

The North American daddylonglegs uses its feet as ears to listen to the chewing of insects inside wood.

In 1978 New York dog-owners started to face $50 fines should their pets discharge their natural functions on the city streets. The fun started when it was realized that the police had to catch the animals in the act.

Did we catch you out? There is no such thing as a Leicester caterpulting spider — but everything else is true!